MAURICE RAVEL

DAPHNIS AND CHLOE

IN FULL SCORE

Dover Publications, Inc.
New York

Daphnis and Chloe

Ballet in 3 Parts

Premiere Performance in Paris at the Théâtre du Châtelet
Russian Season organized by Serge de Diaghilev
(8 June 1912)

CHARACTERS

Chloe	Tamara Karsavina	Daphnis	Vaslav Nijinsky
Lyceion	Frohman	Dorcon	Adolf Bolm
1st Nymph	Marie Piltz	Lammon	Enrico Cecchetti
2nd Nymph	Lubov Tchernicheva	Bryaxis, Leader	
3rd Nymph	Kopatzynska	of the Pirates	Fedorov

Shepherds and Shepherdesses — Pirates — Satyrs
Choir: Sopranos — Altos — Tenors — Basses

Conductor: Pierre Monteux
Choreographed by Michel Fokine
Stage and Costume Design by Léon Bakst

This Dover edition, first published in 1989, is a republication
of *Daphnis et Chloé: Ballet en un acte de Michel Fokine. Musique de
Maurice Ravel*, originally published by Durand & Cie, Paris, in 1913.
The list of instruments and cast of characters have been translated
for this edition, and a glossary of musical terms and a detailed table
of contents (translating the stage directions) have been added.

Manufactured in the United States of America
Dover Publications, Inc., 31 East 2nd Street, Mineola, N.Y. 11501

Library of Congress Cataloging-in-Publication Data

Ravel, Maurice, 1875–1937.
[Daphnis et Chloé]
Daphnis and Chloe.

Ballet; for wordless chorus (SATB) and orchestra.
Reprint. Originally published: Paris : Durand, 1913.
1. Ballets—Scores.   I. Title.
M1520.R26D3   1988   88-753059
ISBN 0-486-25826-2

CONTENTS

1st Part. A meadow at the edge of a sacred wood. In the background, hills. To the right, a grotto, at the entrance of which, hewn out of the rock, is an antique sculpture of three Nymphs. Somewhat toward the background, to the left, a large rock vaguely resembles the form of the god Pan. In the background sheep are grazing. A bright spring afternoon. When the curtain rises, the stage is empty (1). Introduction and Religious Dance. Curtain (1). Youths and girls enter, carrying gifts for the Nymphs in baskets (4). Gradually the stage fills (6). The group bows before the altar of the Nymphs. The girls drape the pedestals with garlands (7). Religious Dance (9). In the far background, Daphnis is seen following his flock (15). Chloe joins him. They proceed toward the altar and disappear at a bend (16). Daphnis and Chloe enter at the foreground and bow down before the Nymphs. The dance ceases (22). Tender emotion on seeing the couple (23). The girls entice Daphnis and dance around him (24). Chloe feels the first twinges of jealousy. At that moment she is swept into the dance of the youths (30). The cowherd Dorcon proves to be especially bold (31). Daphnis in turn seems upset. General Dance (36). At the end of the dance, Dorcon tries to kiss Chloe. She innocently offers her cheek (40). But with an abrupt motion Daphnis pushes aside the cowherd and approaches Chloe affectionately (41). The youths intervene. They position themselves in front of Chloe and gently lead Daphnis away. One of them proposes a dance contest between Daphnis and Dorcon. A kiss from Chloe will be the victor's prize (42). Dorcon's grotesque dance (43). The group sarcastically imitates the clumsy movements of the cowherd . . . (51) . . . who ends his dance in the midst of general laughter (52). Daphnis's light and graceful dance (54). Everyone invites Daphnis to accept his reward (63). Dorcon comes forward as well . . . but he is chased off by the group, accompanied by loud laughter (64). The laughter ceases at the sight of the radiant group formed by the embracing Daphnis and Chloe (65). The group withdraws, taking along Chloe (66). Daphnis remains, immobile, as if in ecstasy (67). Then he lies facedown in the grass, his face in his hands. Lyceion enters (68). She notices the young shepherd, approaches, and raises his head, placing her hands over his eyes. Daphnis thinks this is a game of Chloe's (69). But he recognizes Lyceion and tries to pull away. Lyceion dances (70). As though inadvertently, she drops one of her veils. Daphnis picks it up and places it back on her shoulders. She ironically resumes her dance, which, at first more languorous, becomes steadily more animated until the end (73). Another veil slips to the ground, and is again retrieved by Daphnis. Vexed, she runs off mocking him, leaving the young shepherd very disturbed (75). Warlike sounds and war cries are heard, coming nearer (76). In the middleground, women run across the stage, pursued by pirates (78). Daphnis thinks of Chloe, perhaps in danger, and runs off to save her. Chloe hastens on in panic, seeking shelter (79). She throws herself before the altar of the Nymphs, beseeching their protection. A group of brigands burst onstage, see the girl, and carry her off (81). Daphnis enters looking for Chloe. He discovers on the ground a sandal that she lost in the struggle (82). Mad with despair, he curses the deities who were unable to protect the girl, and falls swooning at the entrance of the grotto (83). An unnatural light suffuses the landscape. A little glow shines suddenly from the head of one of the statues. The Nymph comes to life and descends from her pedestal (84). The second Nymph. The third Nymph (85). They consult together (86) and begin a slow and mysterious dance (87). They notice Daphnis (91). They bend down and dry his tears (92). They revive him and lead him toward the large rock. They invoke the god Pan (93). Gradually the form of the god is outlined (94). Daphnis prostrates himself in supplication. The stage goes dark (95).

2nd Part. Voices are heard from offstage, at first very distant (96). Distant trumpet calls. The voices come nearer (97). A dull glimmer. We are in the pirate camp. Very rugged seacoast. In the background, the sea. To the right and left, a view of large crags. A trireme is seen near the shore. Cypresses here and there. Pirates are seen running to and fro carrying plunder. More and more torches are brought, which finally illuminate the scene violently (98). Bryaxis commands that the captive be brought. Chloe, her hands tied, is led in by two pirates (150). Bryaxis orders her to dance (151). Chloe's dance of supplication (153). She tries to flee (157). She is brought back violently. Despairing, she resumes her dance (158). Again she tries to escape. She is again brought back (162). She abandons herself to despair, thinking of Daphnis (163). Bryaxis tries to carry her off (165). She beseeches (166). The leader carries her off triumphantly (169). Suddenly the atmosphere seems charged with strange elements (170). In various places, lit by invisible hands, little flames flare up (173). Fantastic beings crawl or leap here and there (175). Satyrs appear from every side and surround the brigands (177). The earth opens. The fearsome shadow of Pan is outlined on the hills in the background, making a threatening gesture. Everyone flees in horror (180).

3rd Part. The scene seems to dissolve. It is replaced by the landscape of the 1st Part at the end of the night (182). No sound but the murmur of rivulets produced by the dew that trickles from the rocks (184). Daphnis is still stretched out before the grotto of the Nymphs (185). Gradually the day breaks (187). The songs of birds are heard (188). Far off, a shepherd passes with his flock (196). Another shepherd crosses in the background (199). A group of herdsmen enters looking for Daphnis and Chloe (206). They discover Daphnis and wake him (208). Anxiously he looks around for Chloe (209). She appears at last, surrounded by shepherdesses (210). They throw themselves into each other's arms (211). Daphnis notices Chloe's wreath. His dream was a prophetic vision: The intervention of Pan is manifest (213). The old shepherd Lammon explains that, if Pan has saved Chloe, it is in memory of the nymph Syrinx, whom the god once loved (222). Daphnis and Chloe mime the tale of Pan and Syrinx (223). Chloe plays the young nymph wandering in the meadow (224). Daphnis as Pan appears and declares his love. The nymph rebuffs him (225). The god becomes more insistent (226). She disappears into the reeds. In despair, he picks several stalks to form a flute and plays a melancholy air (227). Chloe reappears and interprets in her dance the accents of the flute (228). The dance becomes more and more animated and, in a mad whirling, Chloe falls into Daphnis's arms (242). Before the altar of the Nymphs, he pledges his love, offering two sheep (250). A group of girls enters dressed as bacchantes, shaking tambourines (251). Daphnis and Chloe embrace tenderly. A group of youths rushes onstage (253). Joyful commotion (254). General dance (258). Daphnis and Chloe (270). Dorcon (274). APPENDIX.

INSTRUMENTATION

Piccolo [Petite Flûte, P^{te} Fl.]
2 Flutes [Grandes Flûtes, G^{des} Fl.]
Alto Flute (G) [Flûte en Sol, Fl. en sol]
2 Oboes [Hautbois, Htb.]
English Horn [Cor Anglais, Cor A.]
E♭ Clarinet [Petite Clarinette en Mi♭, P^{te} Cl.]
2 Clarinets (A, B♭) [Clarinettes en La, Mi♭; Cl.]
Bass Clarinet (B♭) [Clarinette Basse Si♭, Cl. B.]
3 Bassoons (Bassons, B^{ons})
Contrabassoon [Contre-Basson, C. Basson]

4 Horns (F) [Cors chromatiques en Fa, Cors]
4 Trumpets (C) [Trompettes en Ut, Tromp., Trp.]
3 Trombones [Trb.]
Tuba

Timpani [Timbales, Timb.]
Tam-tam
Triangle [Trg.]
Tambourine [Tambour de Basque, T. de B.]
Snare Drum [Caisse Claire, C. Claire, C^{sse} Cl.]
Military Drum [Tambour, Tamb.]
Antique Cymbals [Crotales]
Castanets [Castagnettes, Cast.]

Cymbals [Cymbales, Cymb.]
Wind Machine [Eoliphone, Eoliph.]
Bass Drum [Grosse-Caisse, G. C.]
Celesta [Célesta, Cél.]
Glockenspiel [Jeu de Timbres, J. de Timb., J. de T., Timbres]
Xylophone

2 Harps [Harpes, Hrp.]

Violins I, II [I^{ers} Violons, 1ers V^{ons}, 2^{ds} Violons, 2^{ds} V^{ons}]
Violas [Altos, Alt.]
Cellos [Violoncelles, V^{elles}]
Basses (with low C) [Contrebasses, C.B.]

Piccolo and E♭ Clarinet onstage [sur la scène]
Horn and Trumpet offstage [derrière la scène]

Choir {
Sopranos [Sop.]
Altos [Contraltos, Cont.]
Tenors [Tén.]
Basses [Bas.]
} offstage [derrière la scène]

NB. The CHOIRS can be replaced by the versions provided for that purpose in the orchestral parts.

GLOSSARY

à, au, to, in
accélérez, accelerando
agité, agitez, agitato
ainsi, thus, so on
(en) animant, becoming livelier
animé, lively
animez, accelerando
Appendice, Appendix
assez, fairly
attaque, attack
(en) augmentant, broader
au Mouv^t, a tempo
autres, other, les autres, the others
avant, before
avec, with
avoir, have
baguette, mallet
beaucoup, much
bois, wood
bouches, mouths
ce, this, ces, these
cédez, rallentando
changer en, change to, replace with (winds), retune (timpani)
chefs, first chairs
choeur, choir
commençant, beginning, en commençant par, beginning with
corde, string
court, short
d'abord, at first
danse, dance
davantage, more
de, of
début, beginning
(en) dehors, prominently

dernière, last
derrière, behind, derrière la scène, offstage
doit, doivent, should
du, of the
durant, throughout
en, in, en 3, divisi in 3
encore, again, still
enlevées, removed, enlevez, remove
éponge, sponge
et, and
étouffez, dampen
être, be
exécutions, performances
expressif, expressive
fa, F
fermées, closed
frapper, strike
jeu ordinaire, jeu ord., j. ord., j. o., ordinario, ord.
jusqu'à, jusqu'au, until, up to
la, the
La, A, instrument in A
laisser, allow
langueur, languor
le, les, the
léger, light
légèrement, lightly, slightly
lent, slow, lento
libre, free
loin, far, distant
lumière, light
mailloche, heavy mallet, bass-drum beater
mais, but
même, same
mesure, bar, meter
mettez, attach

mi, E
modéré, moderato
moins, less
monter, raise, retune
mouv^t, tempo, mouv^t du début, tempo primo
ne, not
orchestre, orchestra
ôtez, remove
ouvertes, open
par, by, par pupitre, one desk at a time
(en se) perdant, disappearing
pesant, heavily
peu, little, un peu, a little, peu à peu, gradually
plus, more
pointe, point, tip
pos. nat., ord.
posées, in place
pour, for, in order to
précédente, preceding
prendre, take
prenez, take, change to
près, near
presque, almost
(en) pressant, pressez, stringendo
progressivement, steadily
puis, then
pupitre, desk, stand
ralenti, ralentissez, rallentando
rapide, quick
(en se) rapprochant, coming nearer
ré, D, D string
renversez, reverse
reparaissant, reappearing
réplique, cue
rétablissez, restore, retune

retenu, retenez, meno mosso
revenez, return
rude, harsh, violent
sans, without
scène, stage
séloignant, becoming more distant
servira de, will serve as
seule, alone
si, B
sinon, otherwise
sol, G, G string
son naturel, unstopped, ord.
souple, supple, flexible
sourdine, muted
soutenu, sustained
subit, subito, sudden
suivez, follow
sur, on
temps, beat
tomber, fall
ton, tone, ½ ton, semitone, ton de La, instrument in A
touche, fingerboard
toujours, always, steadily
tous, toute, toutes, all
très, very
un, une, a, une à une, one by one
unis, in unison
ut, C, C string
utiliser, use
vibrer, vibrate, ring
vif, lively
vite, fast
voir, see

DAPHNIS ET CHLOÉ

Une prairie à la lisière d'un bois sacré. Au fond, des collines. A droite, une grotte, à l'entrée
de laquelle, taillées à même le roc, sont figurées trois Nymphes, d'une sculpture archaïque. Un peu
vers le fond, à gauche, un grand rocher affecte vaguement la forme du dieu Pân. Au second plan,
des brebis paissent. Une après-midi claire de printemps. Au lever du rideau, la scène est vide.

Introduction et Danse religieuse

(+) *Lu clarinette basse doit avoir un mi ♭. Sinon prendre le ton de La.*
The bass clarinet should have a B♭. Otherwise use the instrument in A.

La foule s'incline devant l'autel des Nymphes. Les jeunes filles entourent les socles de guirlandes

Un peu retenu

15 Un peu plus lent

Daphnis et Chloé entrent au premier plan et viennent se prosterner devant les Nymphes.

La danse s'interrompt

[16] Mouvᵗ du début

[16] Mouvᵗ du début

Les jeunes filles attirent Daphnis et l'entourent de leurs danses.

Chloé ressent les premières atteintes de la jalousie.   A ce moment, elle est entraînée dans la danse des jeunes gens.

Le bouvier Dorcon se montre particulièrement entreprenant.

26 DANSE GÉNÉRALE

Daphnis à son tour semble dépité.

26 DANSE GÉNÉRALE

51

56
Pte Fl.
Gdes Fl.
Fl. en sol
Htb.
Cor A.
Cl.
Cl. B.
1er et 2e Bons
3e Bon et C.Bon
Sourdines
Cors
Sourdines
1er et 2e Trb.
3e Trb. et Tuba
Timb.
1re Hrp.
2e Hrp.
56
Elle aperçoit le jeune pâtre, s'approche, lui soulève la tête
en lui mettant les mains devant les yeux.
Daphnis croit à une espièglerie de Chloé.
1ers Vons
Div.
2ds Vons
Div.
Alt.
Div.
Vlle Solo
Vlle Solo monter le Sol d'un ½ ton
sur le Sol ♯
p très expressif
rétablissez le Sol ♮
Velles
Div.
Les autres Unis
pizz
C.B.
Div.

Très animé ♩=120

Elle se jette devant l'autel des Nymphes, implorant leur protection.

Très animé ♩=120

Un groupe de brigands fait irruption, aperçoit

Retenu

Elles se penchent et essuient ses larmes

Retenu

sur la touche

Derrière la Scène, on entend des voix, très lointaines d'abord.＊

(1) *La lumière ne reparaissant à l'orchestre qu'une mesure avant* 91 *le Cor derrière la scène servira de réplique pour l'attaque des Violoncelles.*

Since the lights do not come on again in the orchestra until one measure before 91 *, the offstage horn acts as a cue for the cello entrance.*

Une lueur sourde. — On est au camp des pirates. — Côte très accidentée. Au fond, la mer. A droite et à gauche, perspective de rochers. Une trirème se découvre, près de la côte. Par endroits, des cyprès. On perçoit les pirates, courant çà et là, chargés de butin. Des torches sont apportées, qui finissent par éclairer violemment la scène.

100

96
Pte Fl.
Gdes Fl.
Fl. en sol
Htb.
Cor A.
Pte Cl.
Cl.
Cl. B.
1re et 2e Bons
3e Bon C. Bon
Cors
Tromp.
1.2.3.
1re et 2e Trb.
3e Trb. Tuba
Timb.
Trg.
T. de B.
Tamb.
Cymb.
G. C.
1re Hrp.
sol ♯
gliss.
sol ♮
2me Hrp.
ut ♭
ut ♯
1ers Vons Div.
arco
arco.
2ds Vons Div.
pizz.
Alt. Div.
Vlles
Div.
C. B.

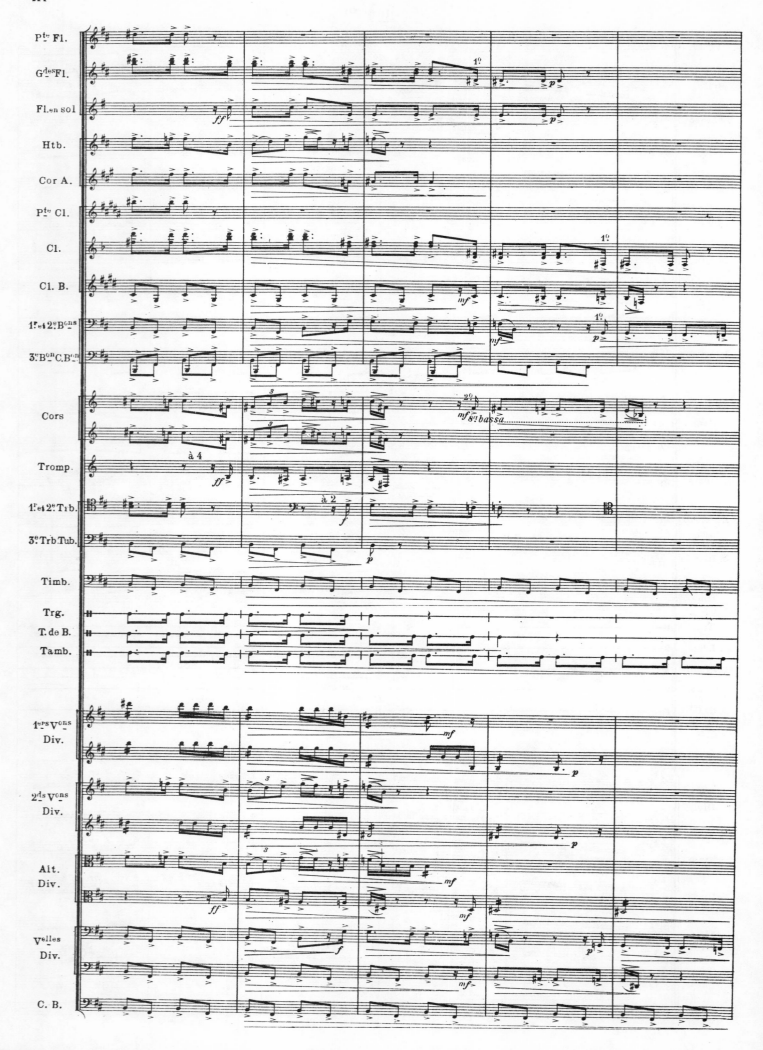

117

106
Ptes Fl.
mf
2e Solo
1o
mf
Gde Fl.
Fl. en sol
Pte Cl.
Cl.
Cl. B.
1er et 2e Bons
3e Bon C.Bon
Cors
Tromp.
1o
pp
3o
pp
Trg.
T. de B.
Cymb.
1re Hrp.
2me Hrp.
106
1ers Vons
Div.
2ds Vons
Div.
Alt.
Div.
Velles
C. B.

118
Fl.
Htb.
Cor A.
Pte Cl.
Cl.
Bons
Cors
Tromp.
1er et 2e Trb.
3e Trb. Tuba
Timb.
Tamb.
Cymb.
G. C.
Célesta
J. de T.
1re Hrp.
2me Hrp.
1ers Vons Div.
2ds Vons Div.
Alt. Div.
Velles Div.
C. B.
à 2
Sourdine
Sourdines
Otez les Sourdines.
Solo
8a bassa

120 Animez peu

126 Un peu moins vif en animant et en augmentant jusqu'à **130**

126 Un peu moins vif en animant et en augmentant jusqu'à **130**

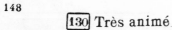

Par endroits, allumés par des mains invisibles de petits feux s'allument

Cà et là, des êtres fantastiques rampent ou sautillent.

Les chèvres-pieds surgissent de toutes parts et entourent les brigands.

de Pân se profile sur les montagnes du fond, dans un geste menaçant. Tous fuient éperdus.

* *Mettez les sourdines une à une en commençant par les chefs de pupitres*
Toutes doivent être posées à **

Attach the mutes one by one beginning with the first stands. All should be in
place by **

3ᵐᵉ PARTIE

153

Derrière la scène très loin

Le décor semble se fondre. Il est remplacé par le paysage de la 1ʳᵉ Partie à la fin de la nuit.

153

184

* Otez les sourdines une à une en commençant par les chefs de pupitres. Toutes doivent être enlevées à 156.

Remove the mutes one by one beginning with the first stands. All should have been removed by 156.

Daphnis est toujours étendu devant la grotte des Nymphes.

188

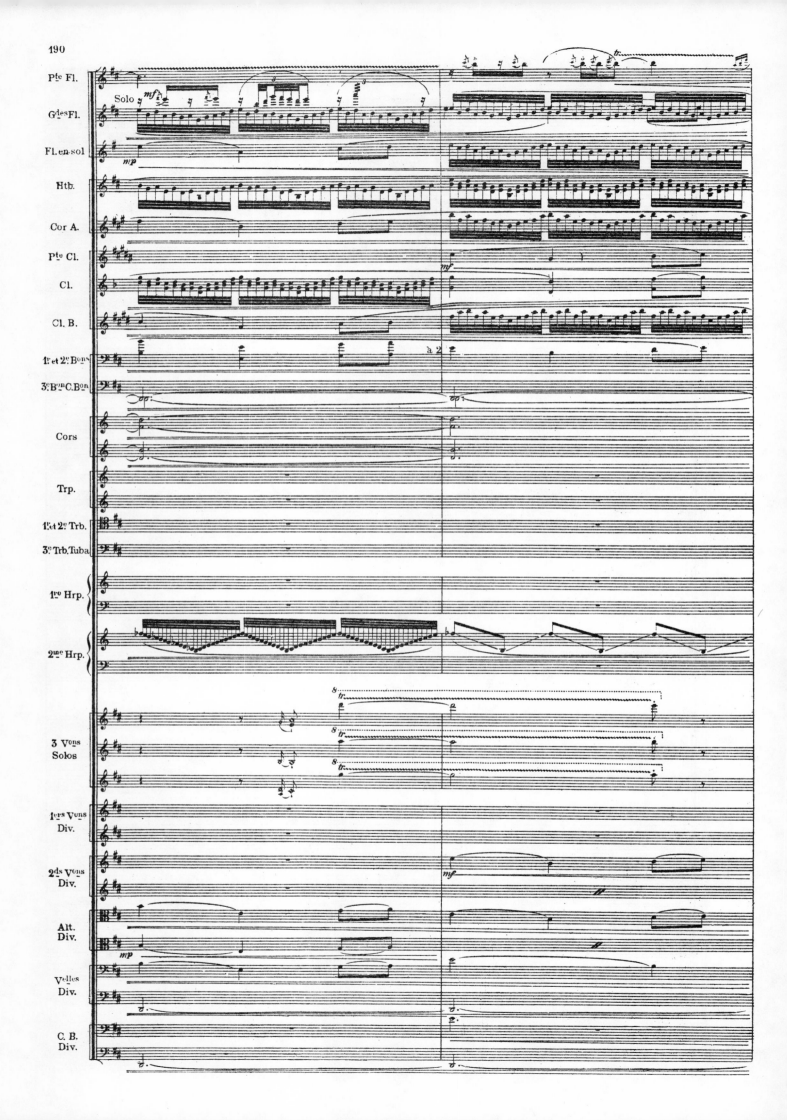

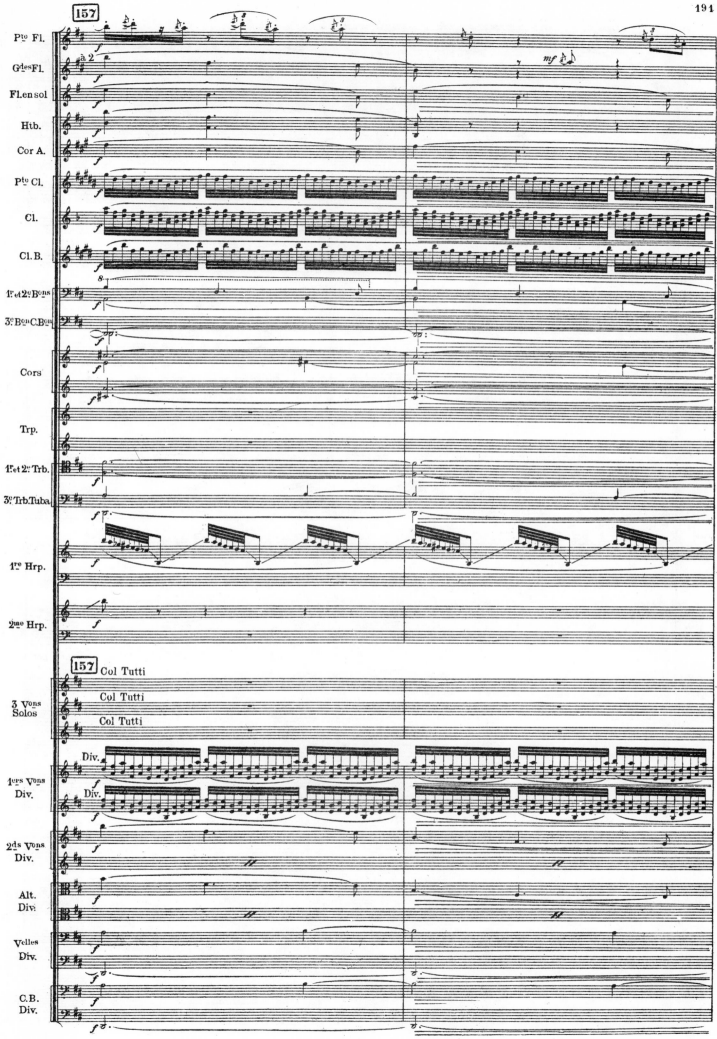

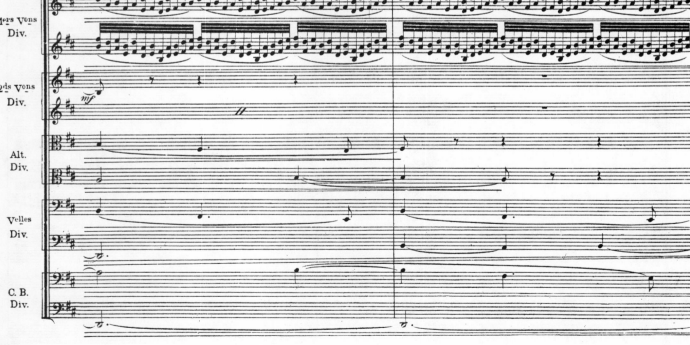

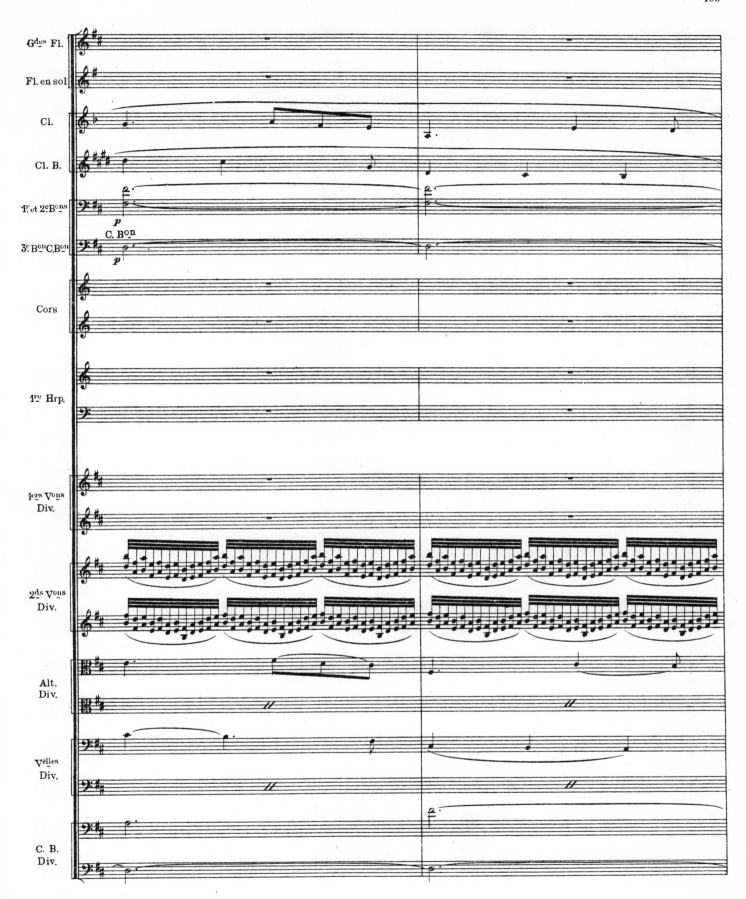

Un autre berger traverse le fond de la scène

en s'éloignant

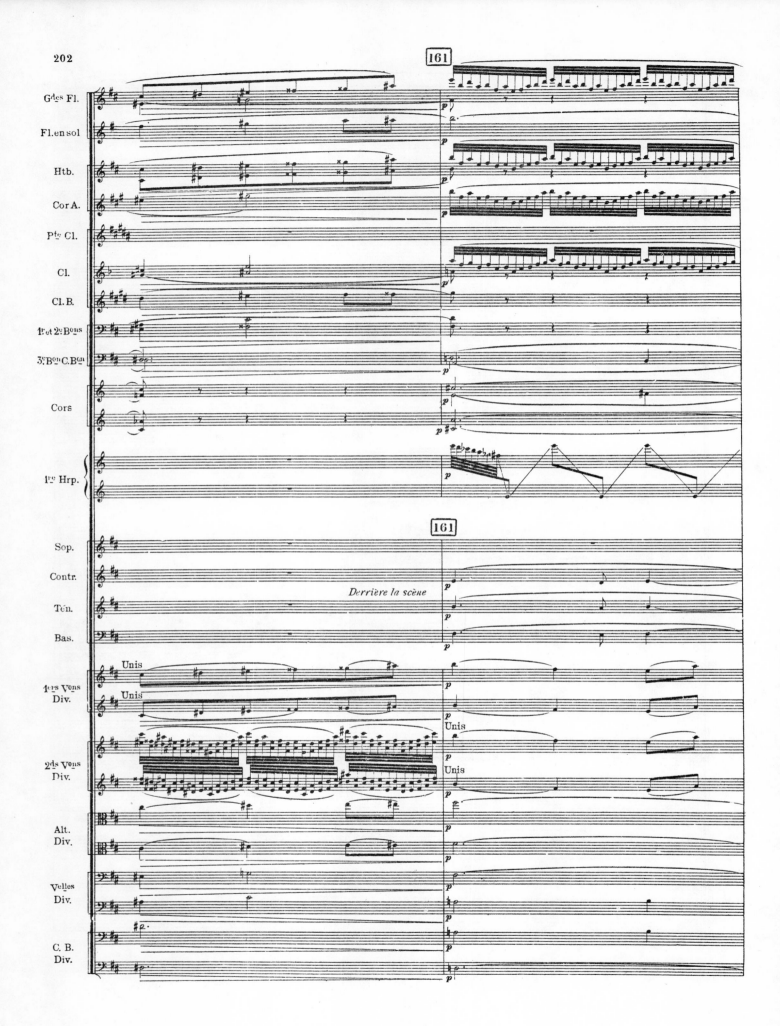

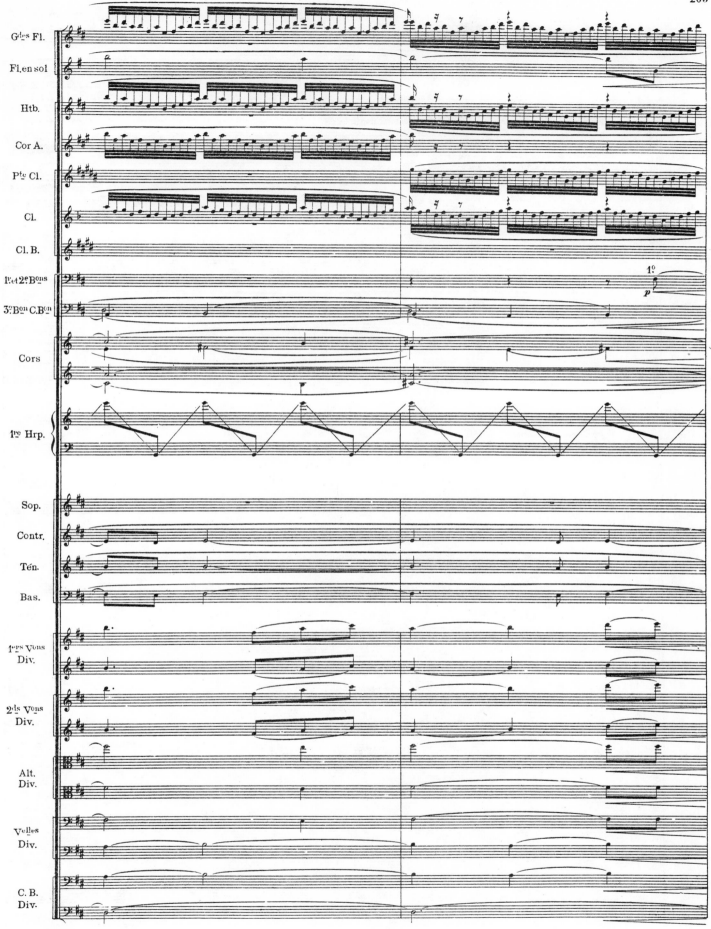

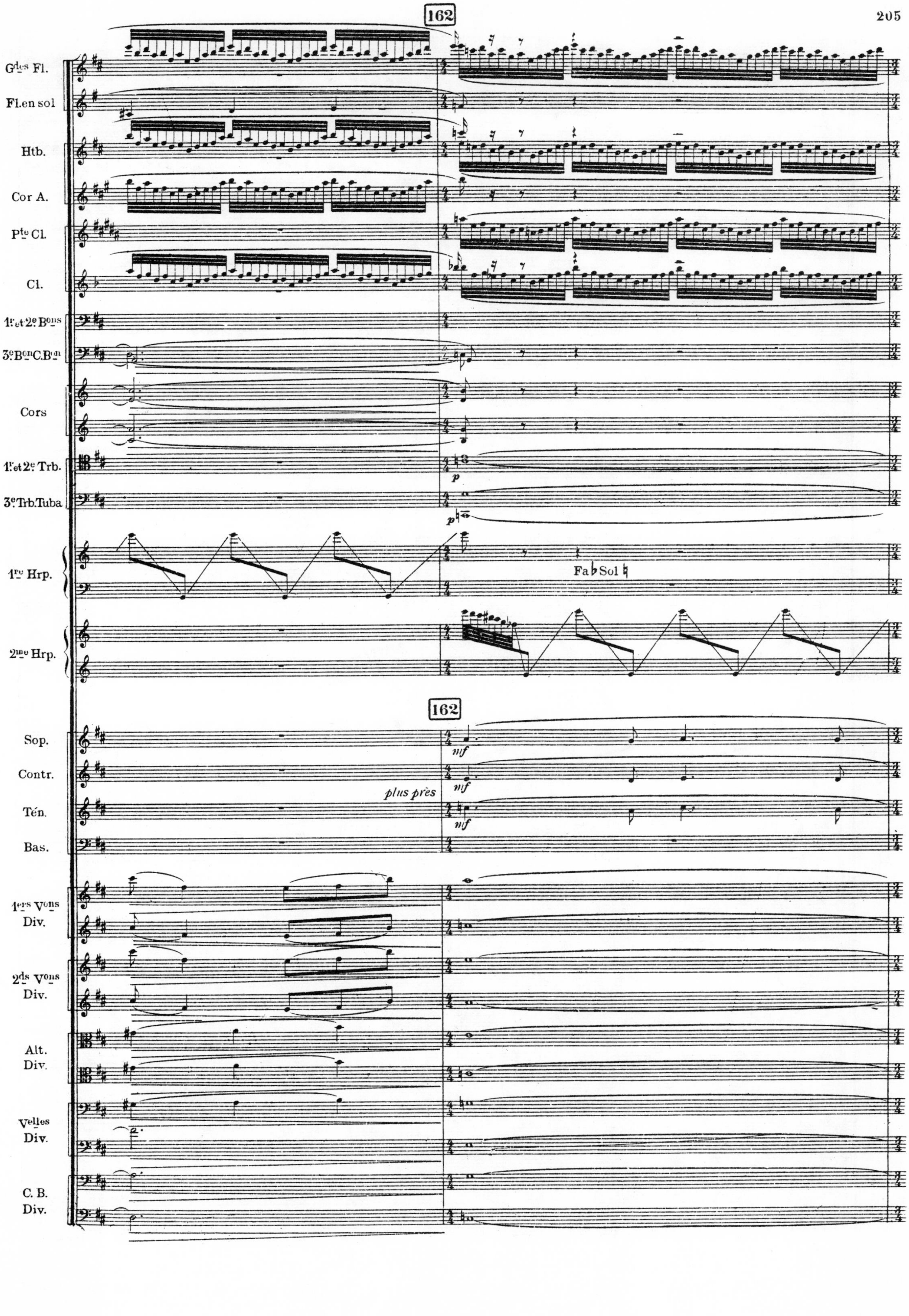
162
Gdes Fl.
Fl. en sol
Htb.
Cor A.
Pte Cl.
Cl.
1r et 2e Bons
3e Bon C. Bon
Cors
1r et 2e Trb.
3e Trb. Tuba
1re Hrp.
Fa♭ Sol♮
2me Hrp.
162
Sop.
Contr.
Tén.
Bas.
plus près
1ers Vons Div.
2ds Vons Div.
Alt. Div.
Velles Div.
C. B. Div.

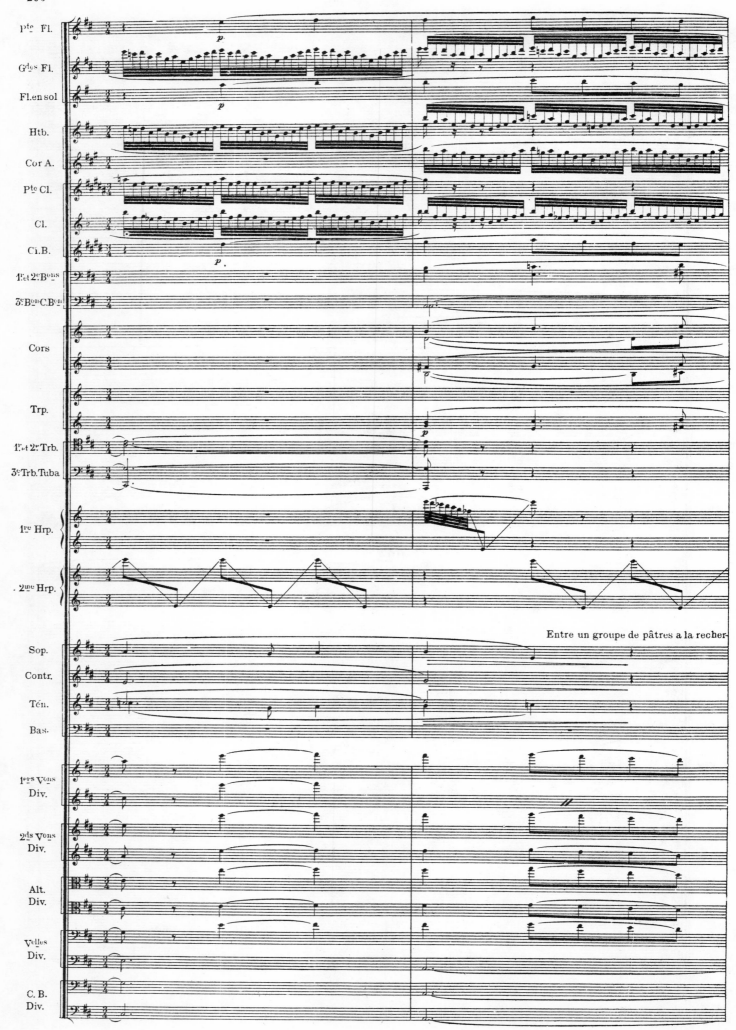

Entre un groupe de pâtres a la recher-

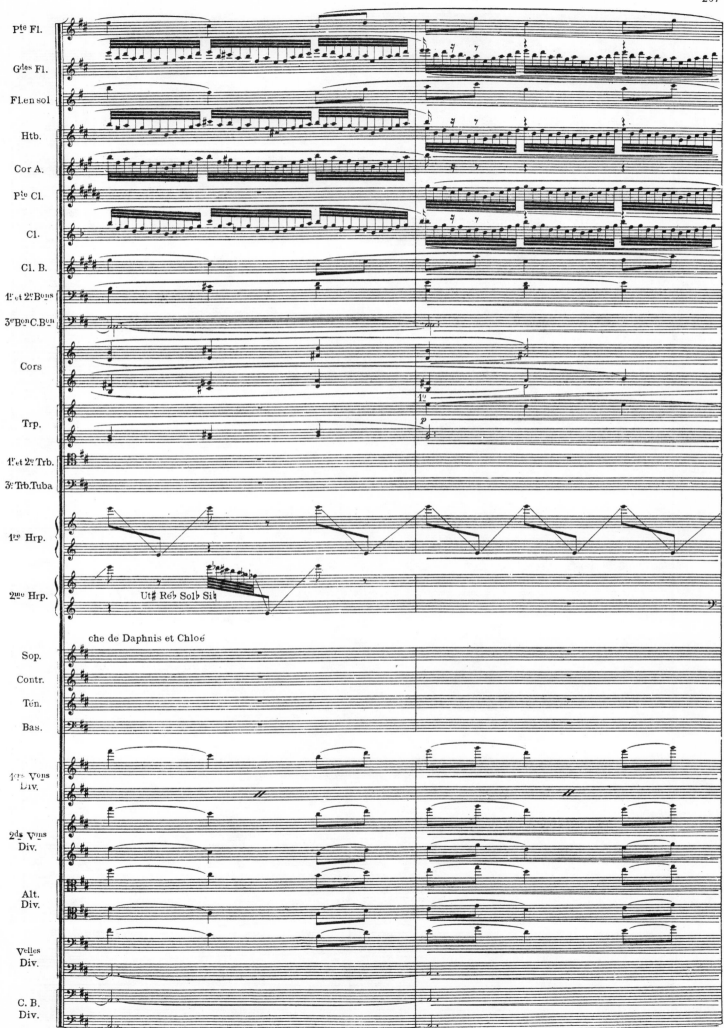

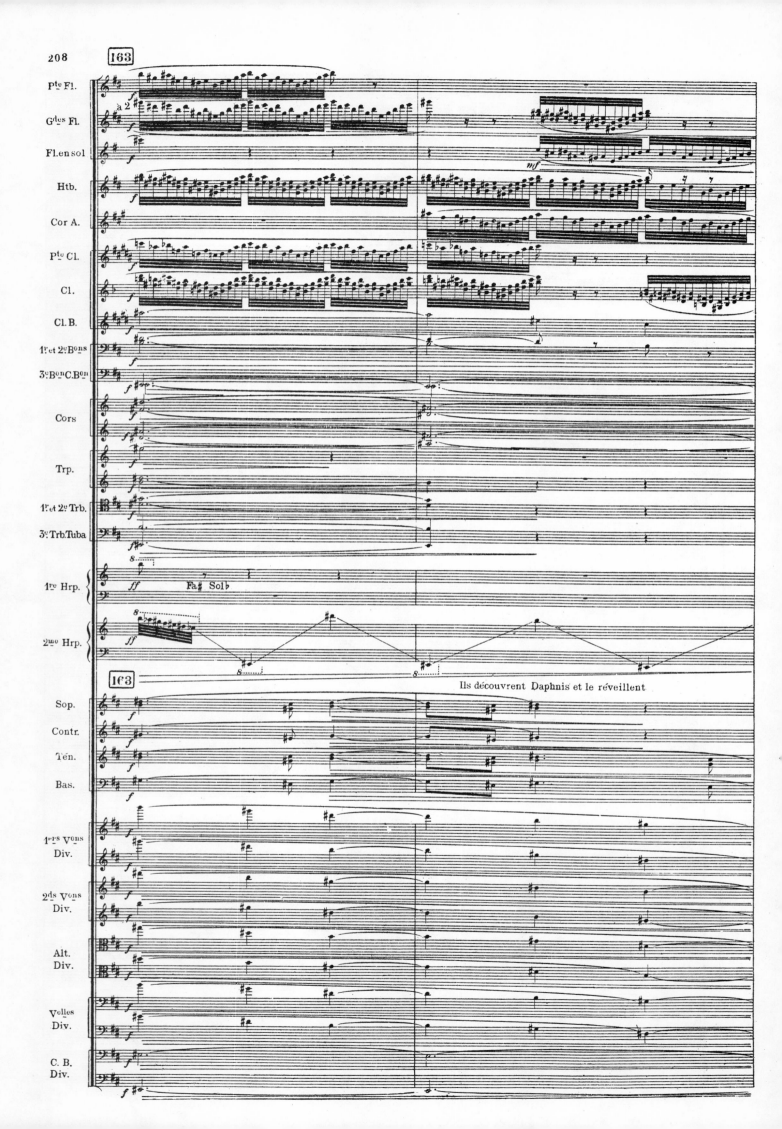

Ils découvrent Daphnis et le réveillent

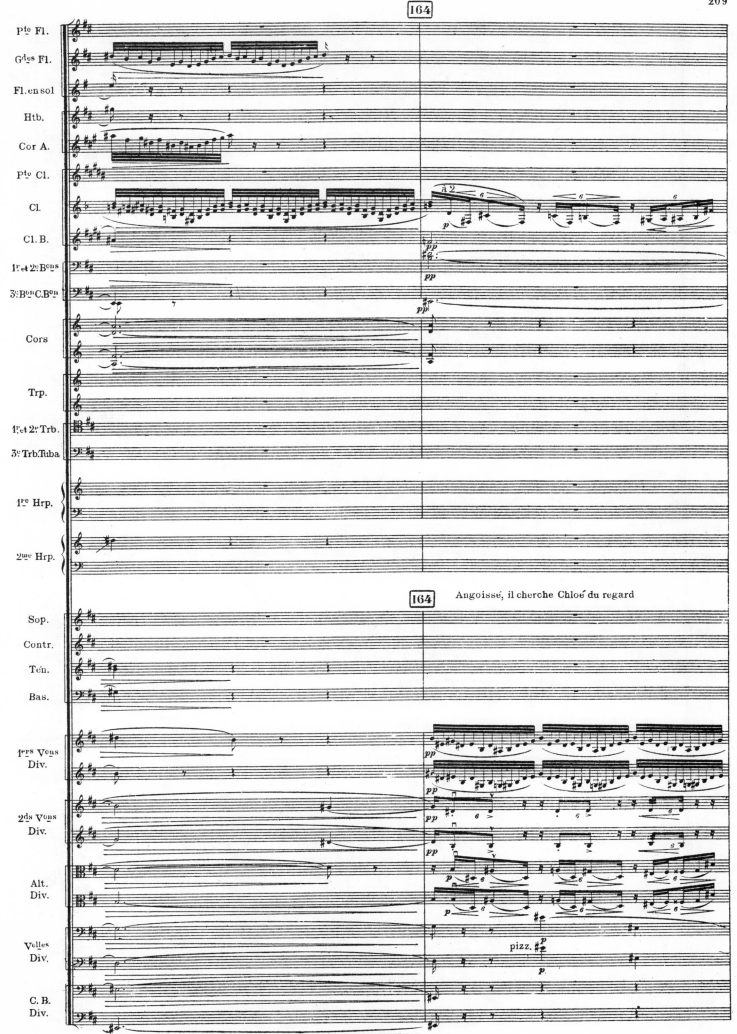

164

164 Angoissé, il cherche Chloé du regard

Elle apparaît enfin, entourée de bergères.

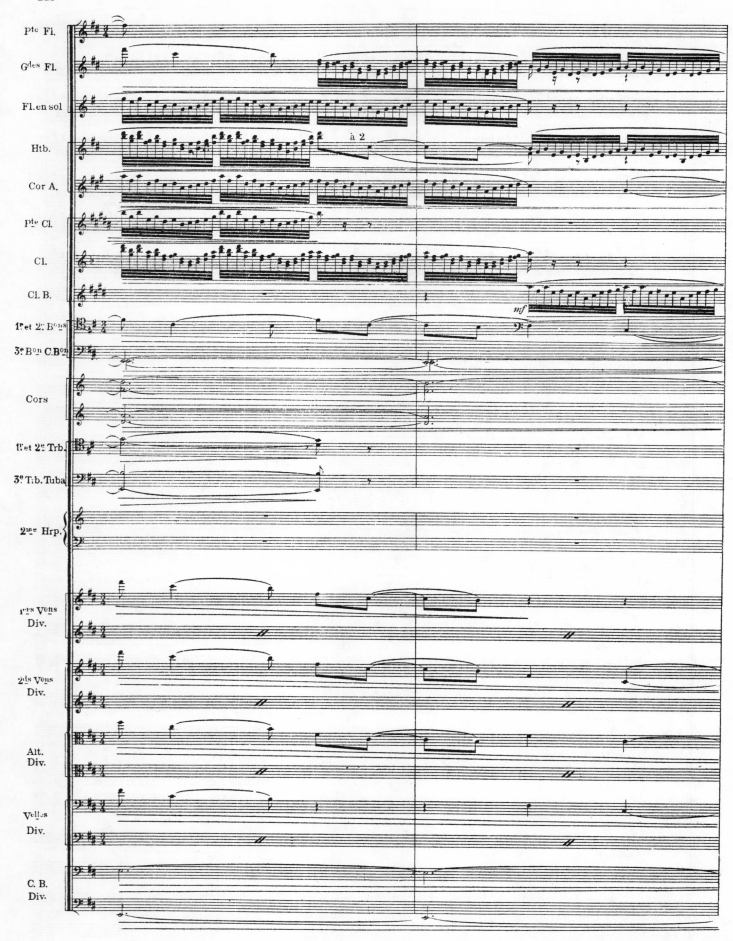

Daphnis aperçoit la couronne de Chloé. Son rêve était une vision

prophétique: L'intervention de Pân est manifeste.

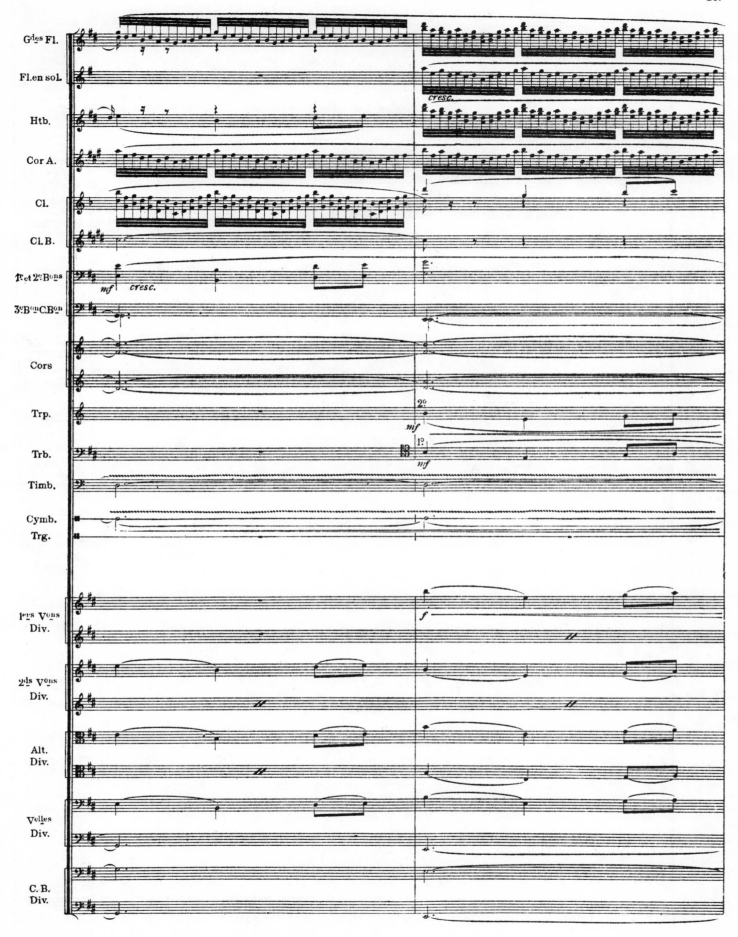

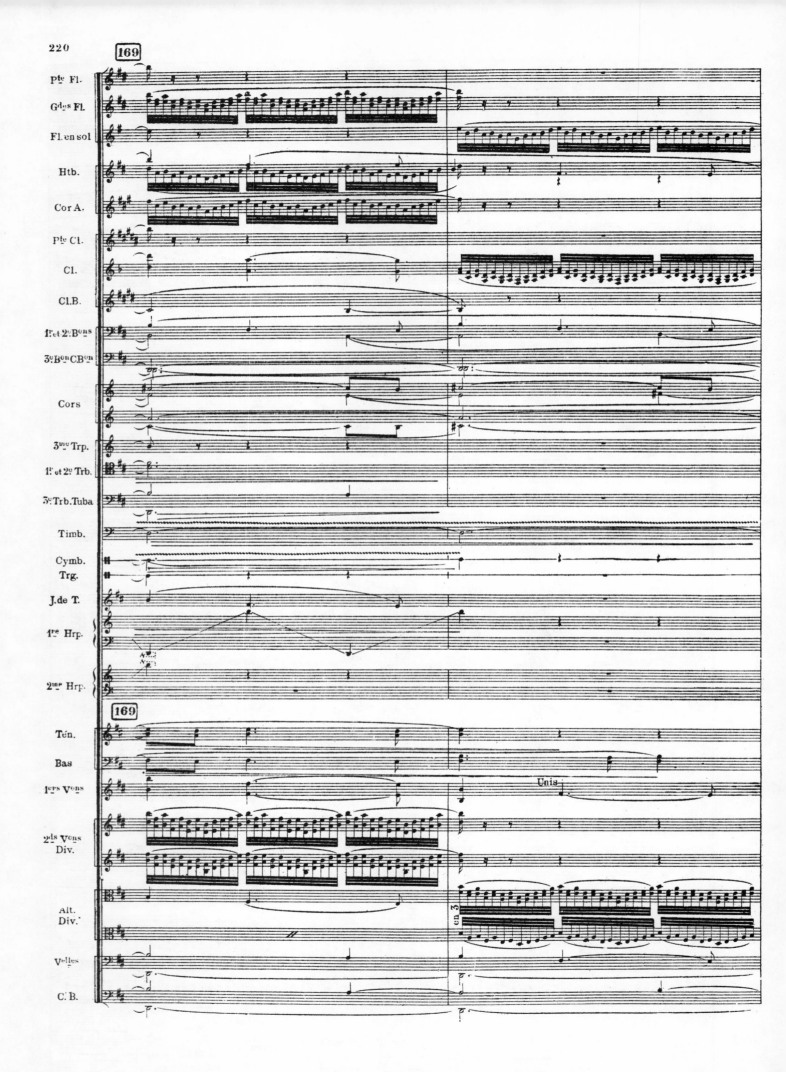

Retenez

222

Le vieux berger Lammon explique que, si Pan a sauvé Chloé, c'est en souvenir de la nymphe Syrinx, dont le dieu fut épris

Daphnis et Chloé miment l'aventure
de Pan et de Syrinx.

Chloé figure la jeune nymphe errant dans la prairie.

Elle disparaît dans les roseaux. Désespéré, il arrache quelques tiges en forme une flûte et joue un air mélancolique.

228

Retenu légèrement   Rall.

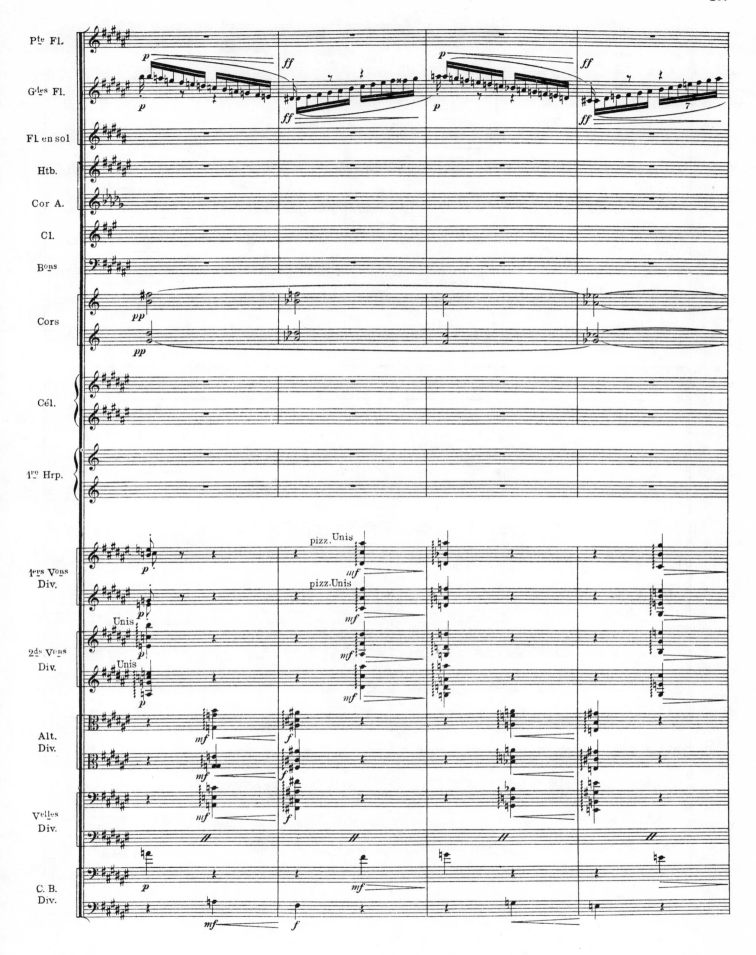

183 En animant toujours davantage

183 En animant toujours davantage

plus en plus et, dans un tournoiement éperdu, Chloé tombe dans les bras de Daphnis

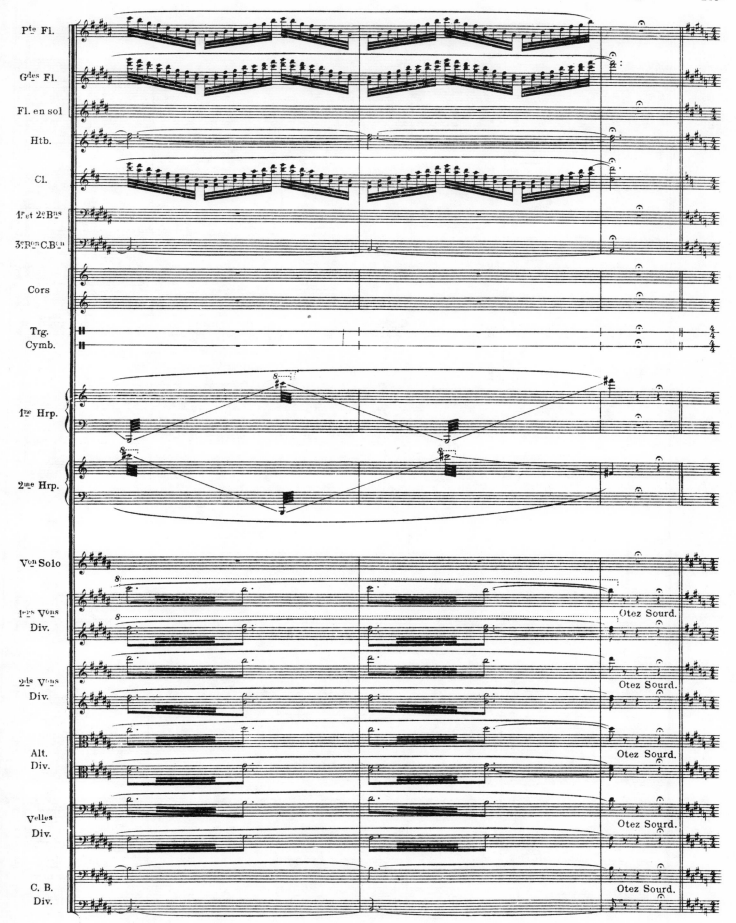

Devant l'autel des Nymphes, il jure sa foi, sur deux brebis.

Entre un groupe de jeunes filles costumées en bacchantes, agitant des tambourins.

Daphnis et Chloé s'enlacent tendrement. Un groupe de jeunes hommes envahit la scène.

Joyeux tumulte.

Ptes Fl.
Gde Fl.
Fl. en sol
Htb.
Cor A.
Pte Cl.
Cl.
Cl. B.
1r et 2e Bons
3e Bon C.Bon
Cors
Trp.
1r et 2e Trb.
3e Trb. Tuba
Timb.
Trg.
Cymb.
Tamb.
Csse Cl.
T. de B.
1re Hrp.
2me Hrp.
1ers Vons Div.
2ds Vons Div.
Alt. Div.
Velles Div.
C. B. Div.
à 2
2e
1o
3e

206
Ptes Fl.
Gdes Fl.
Fl. en sol
Htb
Cor A.
Pte Cl.
Cl.
Cl. B.
1r et 2e Bons
3e Bon C. Bon
à 2
Cors
Trp.
Sourdines
Sourdines 3e
1r et 2e Trb.
3e Trb. Tuba
Cymb.
G. C.
Tamb.
gliss.
2me Hrp.
206
Dorcon
1ers Vons Div.
2ds Vons Div.
pizz.
arco
en 2
en 3
Alt. Div.
Velles Div.
C. B. Div.

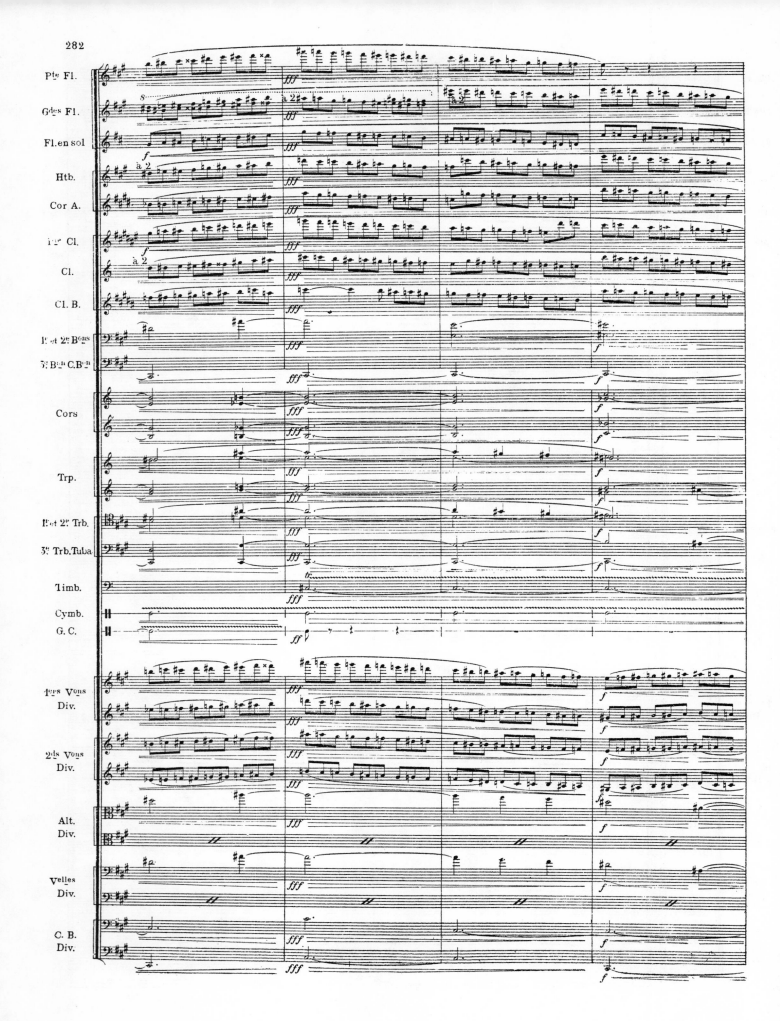

284

211
Gdes Fl.
Fl. en sol
Cor A.
Cl.
Cl. B.
1er et 2e Bons
3e Bon C. Bon
Cors
Trp.
1re et 2e Trb.
Csse Cl.
Cél.
1re Hrp.
2me Hrp.
1ers Vons Div.
2ds Vons Div.
Alt. Div.
Velles Div.
C. B. Div.
à 2
mf
p
pp
pizz.
arco
sur le sol
gliss.
tr
2o
4o

212
Gdes Fl.
Fl. en sol
Htb.
Cl.
Cl. B.
1r et 2e Bons
3e Bon C.Bon
Cors
otez les Sourdines
Trp.
3o
4e
1r et 2e Trb.
Csse Cl.
Cél.
1re Hrp.
Ut♭ Ré♭ Mi♭ Fa♮
Sol♭ La♭ Si♭
2me Hrp.
Div.
212
Unis
arco
1ers Vons
Div.
sur le ré
arco
gliss
2ds Vons
Div.
sur l'ut
gliss
Alt.
Div.
Velles
Div.
C. b.
Div.

213
Gdes Fl.
Fl.en sol
Htb.
à 2
pp
Cl.
Cl. B.
1r et 2e Bons
2º
3e Bon C.Bon
Cors
Trp.
Trg.
Cymb.
Tamb.
Csse Cl.
Cast.
T. de B.
ppp
1re Hrp.
Sop.
Contr.
Tén.
Bas.
213
1ers Vons
Div.
2ds Vons
Div.
Div.
Alt.
Div.
Velles
Div.
C.B.
Div.
p

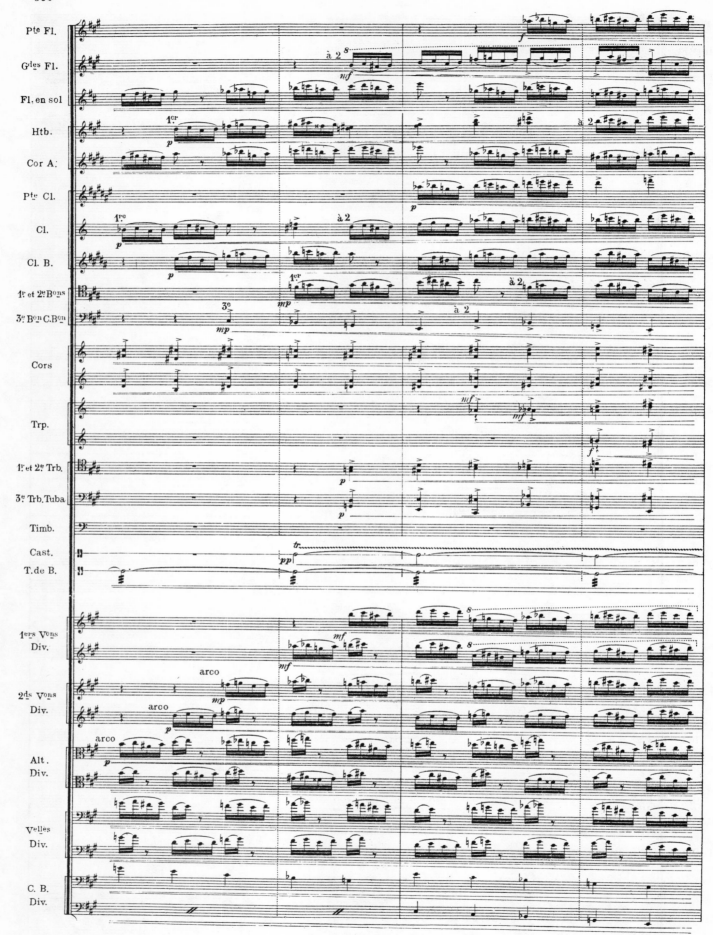